THE GOLDEN YEARS

1958

text: David Sandison

design: Paul Kurzeja

SIENA

A year of firsts, of remarkable come-backs, of notable scandals and at least one unforgettable tragedy, 1958 was a memorable period in modern history, as you'll discover (or be reminded) as you dip into its news and events.

First, the firsts: We saw the first crossing of the Antarctic over land, and the first crossing under the Arctic by submarine. Arnold Palmer won his first US Masters, and the world caught its first glimpse of a revolutionary craft which could travel on land and sea. The people of Aldermaston witnessed their first rally by thousands of supporters of an organisation called The Campaign for Nuclear Disarmament, and many thousands more tuned into the first screenings of a British TV show which showed rock 'n' roll the way it really was - non-stop, loud and brash.

Come-back of the year had to be the return from self-imposed political exile of General Charles de Gaulle, France's saviour in WWII.

Running him a close second was Cuba's rebel leader, Fidel Castro. Reported dead a year ago, Castro proved he was alive, well - and determined to rid his country of the corrupt Batista regime. His come-back began in earnest as his troops moved into action.

Scandals don't come any bigger than the two which dominated headlines in 1958 - the shock discovery

that the 13 year old girl who accompanied rock 'n' roll hero Jerry Lee Lewis on his first British tour was his new bride, and that the person who stabbed actress Lana Turner's gangster boyfriend to death on Oscars night was her teenaged daughter.

1958 saw the arrival of a new Pope, a successor to the legendary Christian Dior, and the departure from the public stage (for two years, anyway) of Elvis Presley, Uncle Sam's newest army recruit.

The tragedy was, of course, the Munich air crash which killed so many of a young Manchester United team most people believed were on the verge of proving themselves one of the world's best-ever soccer club sides.

Fuchs Beaten By Hillary In Race To South Pole

A BRITISH ANTARCTIC expedition, led by explorer-adventurer Dr Vivian Fuchs   arrived at the South Pole today by a 2,100 mile overland route, to be welcomed by the rival New Zealand team of Everest hero Sir Edmund Hillary, which had beaten them to becoming the first party to repeat Robert Scott's 1912 South Pole trek by 17 days.

The snow tractors of Hillary's team had arrived at the permanent American scientific base at the Pole after what its leader described as 'a hell-bent dash' from its final depot. They had set out from Scott Base on McMurdo Sound while the British - who are attempting the first-ever trans-Antarctic crossing, with the South Pole their midway target - came from Shackleton Base on the Vansee Sea.

British progress during their eight-week journey was adversely affected by soft snow, bad weather, precipitous crevasses and the loss of four of their nine tracked vehicles and snow-sleds with mechanical problems.

Although rivalry between the two expeditions was naturally fierce, the meeting of Hillary and Fuchs' teams set off a joint celebration party. After a brief rest and repair stop, the Brits began the second half of their mission, which was successfully completed on March 2 when they arrived at Scott Base.

Fuchs (left) and Hillary at the South Pole

Chancellor Quits Cabinet In Money Policy Row

Although he described them as 'little local difficulties', British Prime Minister Harold Macmillan was obviously shaken by the resignations of his Chancellor of the Exchequer and two Treasury Ministers after the Cabinet supported Macmillan's refusal to peg next year's government spending at existing levels.

Leaving London for a Commonwealth tour, Macmillan responded coolly to press calls for a comment on the departure of Chancellor Peter Thorneycroft and Treasury ministers Enoch Powell and Nigel Birch.

'I thought that the best thing to do was to settle up these little local difficulties and then turn to the wider vision of the Commonwealth', he said.

Sputnik Disintegrates In Earth's Atmosphere

Sputnik-I, the man-made satellite launched last October to give the USSR a lead over the United States in the space race, broke up today as it re-entered the earth's atmosphere, Soviet scientists confirmed.

The satellite, which was said to be a 22-inch diameter sphere weighing 83.6 kg - six times heavier than the satellite which the US plan to launch some time this year - had maintained an 18,000 mph orbit some 500 miles above the earth. With two transmitters aboard, it had emitted an unbroken stream of signals which many amateur radio enthusiasts had been able to pick up.

Soviet triumph was enhanced by the successful launch and safe return in November of a second satellite containing Laika, a young dog. That satellite was even heavier than Sputnik-I, being packed with food and water supplies for its passenger and a range of apparatus to measure cosmic rays and conditions in space.

Increased concern at the Soviet lead was reflected in Washington on January 7 when Texas Senator Lyndon B. Johnson called for extra expenditure to ensure that the US overtake the Russians.

JANUARY 30

Yves St Laurent Assumes Dior's Couture Crown

The King is dead - long live the King! French fears that the gap left by the death of Christian Dior, in October last year, would leave Paris without a major international couturier, ended today with the first brilliant collection of 23 year old Yves St Laurent. Response to the former law student's show - star centre-piece of which was his 'trapeze line' look - was so enthusiastic that the huge crowd which gathered outside his salon would not disperse until the new 'sovereign' made an appearance on a balcony. St Laurent's rise is all the more remarkable because the bulk of his début collection was designed and created at his mother's home in Algeria, the only space he could use for nothing!

Seven Killed, Hundreds Hurt As Cyprus Turks Riot

THE RELATIVELY PEACEFUL Cypriot Turkish community turned to angry violence today after a British Army Land Rover drove at speed through a demonstration to spark off riots which left seven people dead and hundreds injured. Order was only regained after an appeal by Turkish leader Rauf Denktash, the island's one-time Solicitor-General.

The original incident happened in Nicosia and turned what had been an orderly and well-behaved demo in support of greater political links between Cyprus and Turkey into an enraged mob. Despite the introduction of an immediate curfew by the British governor, Sir Hugh Foot, thousands of Turks took to the streets, setting tobacco factories, stores and garages ablaze, overturning and burning police vehicles, and stoning security forces who tried to restore order.

During the last two years of unrest in Cyprus, the Turkish community - though agitating strongly for increased links with their homeland - has maintained far greater order than the Greek population, whose EOKA terrorist organization has carried out a murderous bombing and arson campaign to support calls for an end to British rule and union with Greece. Today's events are therefore an ominous change in the pattern of political life on this embattled and embittered island.

Ten Die In Dagenham Train Crash

British Rail promised a full inquiry today when 10 people died and 80 others were injured in a train crash at Dagenham, the Essex town some 20 miles east of London. Coming, as it did, only a month after the Lewisham tragedy in which 92 rail passengers were killed and 200 injured when two trains collided in heavy fog, the Dagenham crash has resulted in widespread and renewed calls for the whole question of rail safety in Britain to be reviewed and revised.

Mongolian Quake Creates New Landscape

Soviet scientists today released first details of the effects of last month's massive Mongolian earthquake, believed to have been the biggest to hit the region in living memory.

According to information presented in Moscow, the quake actually shifted and altered mountains, and created whole new valleys. A number of new rivers are also reported to have sprung up in the region, while the courses of others have been drastically changed.

FEB

Soccer World Mourns As Munich Crash Claims Busby Babes

THE INTERNATIONAL SPORTING community joined with the people of Manchester in mourning today as news spread of the deaths of seven 'Busby Babes' - the brilliant young Manchester United team created by manager Matt Busby - when the plane carrying them home crashed on take-off from a snow-covered Munich airport. Eight journalists travelling with the team were also killed, as were three members of the club's staff.

Matt Busby, whose vision created what many believe was the greatest-ever British club squad, was one of those critically injured in the crash, which happened as they returned from their most recent victory, in Belgrade, which had won them a place in the European Cup semi-finals.

Four of the players whose bodies were recovered from the wreckage of the BEA Ambassador were full internationals - captain Roger Byrne (28), who'd made the English left-back position his own for every match since 1954, outside-left David Pegg (22), who'd won his first England cap last May, 25 year old Tommy Taylor, 18 times England's centre-forward, and four-time Irish Republic inside-right, the 22 year old Bill Whelan.

The other player fatalities were right-half Eddie Colman (21), 24 year old centre-half Mark Jones and Geoff Bent

(25). One of the press team killed was former English international goal-keeper Frank Swift.

Among those worst injured were Matt Busby and England internationals Bill Foulkes, John Berry and the big left-half Duncan Edwards, who would die on February 21.

The crash occurred after the aircraft had stopped to refuel at Munich. After one aborted attempt to take off on the ice-covered runway, the crew decided to try a second time. This time the plane went into a slide, hitting a fence and an airport building before breaking in two.

Main picture: Manchester United line up before their match with Red Star in Belgrade. Insert: Matt Busby in an oxygen tent at Munich Hospital

CND Formed To End UK Nuclear Arms - Mac Reveals Missile Bases

A powerful new protest group - The Campaign for Nuclear Disarmament (CND) - was formed at a London meeting this evening. Created to pressure the British government to abandon nuclear weapons, it promised a muscular and energetic pursuit of its objectives which included an immediate end to nuclear bomb tests by British scientists.

CND's birthplace was Westminster's Central Hall, the conference centre which stands within view of the Houses of Parliament and was the venue for the inaugural session of the newly-founded United Nations in 1946.

Headed by a committee which included Nobel Prize-winning philosopher Bertrand Russell, Labour MP Michael Foot, left-wing journalist James Cameron and best-selling author JB Priestley, CND was created out of the year-old National Council for Abolition of Nuclear Weapon Tests. This had attracted thousands to a series of regional protest meetings, during the course of which it became clear that a huge number of people believed Britain should drop out of the nuclear weapons business altogether.

Battle lines were drawn on February 24 when Prime Minister Harold Macmillan announced that US missiles - many believed to pack a nuclear punch - were to be based in Yorkshire, Lincolnshire and East Anglia. Although they will be sited at RAF stations, American servicemen will manage their installation and maintenance.

FEBRUARY 8

Lean and Guinness Triumph As 'River Kwai' Wins 3 BAFTA Awards

A suitably glittering gala night in London gave director David Lean and actor Alec Guinness a chance to practise the acceptance speeches everyone predicts they'll have to make at next month's Oscars ceremony when they collect the same category prizes they won at this year's British Academy of Film and Television Arts (Bafta) awards dinner.

To no-one's great surprise, their smash hit movie The Bridge On The River Kwai was voted Best Picture by Bafta members. Lean was awarded the Best Director prize, and Alec Guinness' gripping portrayal of the stiff-lipped English colonel PoW (pictured above) ordered to build a rail bridge by his Japanese captors, earned him a walk-over Best Actor title.

Triumph And Disaster Mark US Entry In Space Race

THE UNITED STATES entered the space race proper today when Explorer, its 30lb satellite, was successfully launched from Florida's Cape Canaveral to begin orbiting the earth at altitudes ranging from 230 to 2,000 miles.

The launch was an especial triumph for the US team led by Werner von Braun, chief scientist of Nazi Germany's wartime V-2 rocket bomb project, following the dramatic launch-pad explosion which ended their first attempt last December.

Today's launch was achieved with a modified military Jupiter C rocket which lifted the satellite free of the earth's gravitational pull. Packed with miniaturized apparatus, Explorer was to monitor a number of space phenomena for ground-based scientists.

US triumph was short-lived, however. On February 20, an Atlas rocket blew up at Cape Canaveral during launch countdown. It was the fifth failed launch in seven attempts, and raised serious questions about American readiness to compete with the Soviets, already two major leaps ahead with Sputnik-I and Laika's space journey.

Race Ace Fangio In Cuban Kidnap Riddle

Hostage dramas are no rarity in the hot-bed of intrigue which is South American and Caribbean politics, with equal measures of publicity and ransom money the prize for those responsible for successful kidnaps. But events in the Cuban capital, Havana, today were pretty bizarre.

The hostage seized by Cuban rebels was no less than the holidaying Argentinian world motor racing champion, Juan Fangio - a high-profile catch for the forces of socialist guerrilla Fidel Castro, and one calculated to produce world headlines to help publicize their war with Cuban dictator Fulgencio Batista, let alone a hefty cash injection to their coffers if and when their ransom demands were met.

Mystery surrounds events of the next 28 hours. It's still not clear if a ransom was paid (and, if so, how much), or whether Castro ordered Fangio's release when he realized the resultant publicity was negative. Either way, Fangio was a free man by the following evening, and headed away from Cuba to the comparitive safety of Miami and the 1958 motor racing season.

Lord Chancellor Bans Beckett's Blasphemous 'Endgame'

No stranger to controversy at the best of times, the Irish-born, Paris-based playwright Samuel Beckett - probably best known for his surreal Waiting For Godot - found himself a member of the select band of artists the Lord Chancellor decided to deny a licence. The work in question was Beckett's new play Endgame. The Lord Chancellor demanded the removal of lines he considered blasphemous. Beckett refused to make the cuts, so the only people who could see his typically-oblique and often perplexing offering were those who belonged to a theatre club which excluded the general public.

Teen Idol Elvis Becomes US PFC 53310761

A FULL MEDIA CIRCUS was on hand at the US Army's Draft Board office in Memphis, Tennessee today when Elvis Presley arrived to say goodbye to two years as one of the world's most successful entertainers, to his luxuriant locks and to the jet-set lifestyle his fame had created. As flashbulbs popped and television cameras whirred, his $1000 a week pocket money allowance changed to an $83.20 per month pay cheque and he was told he'd be going to Fort Chaffee, Arkansas, for his induction and then to Fort Hood, Texas, for basic training with the 2nd Armored Division.

Confronted with the reality of a two-year Presley absence as the 23 year old rock superstar followed his patriotic duty as Private First Class US53310761 Presley, Elvis A, many of the hundreds of fans who surrounded the draft centre were sobbing inconsolably. That grief increased the next day when, under the ever-watchful eye of his manager, 'Colonel' Tom Parker, a barber gave America's newest grunt a regulation short back and sides.

Elvis' sign-on had been delayed to enable him to finish filming King Creole, his fourth movie, and build up a stockpile of new recordings which RCA Records could use to fill the gap while their goldmine was away. The singer had made it clear that he intended to take his military service seriously. There would be no shows while he was a soldier - he'd even turned down the option of remaining an entertainer with the Army's Special Services Division.

Giving a rueful smile as he surveyed the barber's work in a mirror, Presley told pressmen: 'I think it will be a great experience for me'. At least he didn't sing his latest hit as the clippers went to work. It's called Don't.

Sobers Smashes An Unbeaten 365 To Set New Test Record

A memorable day in cricketing history as 21 year-old West Indies batsman Garfield Sobers broke the 28 year Test record of Sir Leonard Hutton when he scored a simple single in Kingston, Jamaica to take his personal score to 365. As thousands of the 20,000 crowd raced on to the pitch to help carry their local hero shoulder-high to the pavilion, the West Indies declared at the very useful total of 790 for three, setting their Pakistani opponents a mountainous and impossible obstacle.

Sobers' feat was remarkable in every way.

Not only did he beat the 364 record set by Hutton against Australia at the Oval in 1938, and do it in three hours less than the 13 hours-plus it had taken the Englishman, it also marked Sobers' first Test century.

The Pakistani tour had already gone into the record books. Back in January, Hanif Mohammed, Pakistan's 24 year old opening batsman, smashed Hutton's record of 13hr 20mins at the crease, set in that run-scoring bonanza in 1938. While Hanif had failed to beat the score record with his 337, he did bat for a marathon 16hr 13mins.

Suffragette Leader Dame Christabel Dies

MARCH 14

Dame Christabel Pankhurst, eldest daughter of Britain's suffragette leader, Emily Pankhurst, who - with her mother and sisters Sylvia and Adela - founded the Women's Social and Political Union in 1903 to fight for women's political rights, died today, aged 78.

A heroine of the movement to win women the vote, Christabel was an enthusiastic supporter of the decision to increase the WSPU's militancy when their initially lawful actions were stonewalled. Adopting more extreme tactics, including attacking politicians and policemen, and chaining themselves to lamp-posts and railings, the suffragettes endured repeated prison sentences and forced feeding. Diverting their efforts to aiding Britain's war efforts during WWI, the Pankhursts reformed the suffrage movement as The Women's Party in 1918, fielding 16 unsuccessful candidates but winning the vote for women over the age of 30.

MARCH 27

Khrushchev Emerges As Soviet Supremo

NIKITA KHRUSHCHEV became the Soviet Union's undisputed leader today when, in a simple administrative manoeuvre, he ousted his long-time colleague and rival, Prime Minister Nikolai Bulganin.

By adopting the toppled Bulganin's job and retaining the all-important job of Communist Party Secretary, Khrushchev occupied the two most powerful posts in the USSR - something only the dictator Josef Stalin had done before, during WWII. His move ended the double act which had become a dominant feature of international affairs, with the sombre and goatee bearded Bulganin playing straight man to

Khrushchev's more ebullient, though always shrewd, showman.

Long recognized as little more than Khrushchev's yes-man, the former secret policeman, Mayor of Moscow and Minister of Defence, was toppled by the addition of his name to those of the 'anti-party group' of Molotov, Malenkov and Kaganovitch who'd tried to topple Khrushchev in June 1957. Khrushchev would not be content with merely taking the 62 year old Bulganin's title from him. Within five months, Bulganin would lose his seat on the Party Presidium and retire from political life to become chairman of the Soviet State Bank.

MARCH 12

Batista Suspends Constitution To Fight Castro

Cuba's President Fulgencio Batista stepped up his fight against the increasingly-popular and successful rebel army of former student leader Fidel Castro today when he suspended his island state's constitution. With the freedom to carry out whatever moves he feels are necessary to wipe out Castro, his forces and any he believes are sympathetic to Castro's socialist movement.

Castro, a former student activist once

imprisoned for leading opposition to Batista's corrupt Mafia-backed regime, returned to Cuba almost two years ago after spending three years in Mexico receiving military training. Since then his ever-growing army of skilled militia and peasant recruits had harassed and disrupted police and army positions in rural areas and built a strong following among disenchanted students.

A powder keg had been lit.

MARCH 25

Fifth Title Victory Is Sweet For Sugar Ray

A points victory over title-holder Carmen Basilio in Chicago tonight gave the legendary 'Sugar' Ray Robinson an especially sweet taste of success.

Not only had he regained the world middleweight title the hard-hitting Basilio had taken from him last September in a controversial split decision fight, but by doing so he'd become champ for a record-breaking fifth time.

Now aged 37, the Detroit-born genius had been world welterweight champion between 1946 and 1951, relinquishing it after five successful defences to win the middleweight crown of his long-time rival Jake LaMotta. His win tonight was vindication of his decision, in 1955, to come out of the retirement he'd announced after being beaten by Joey Maxim in 1952.

Debs Presented At Palace For The Last Time

The debutantes who processed past the Queen at Buckingham Palace today, making their nervous curtsies as they 'came out' into society, knew they were making history. The tradition of presentation at Court for the daughters of British aristocrats and other society bigwigs, was to be scrapped, with today's ceremony the very last the Queen was prepared to undertake.

While Prince Philip was widely accepted as having suggested the ceremony was an archaic practice, the Queen was said to have readily accepted the view that it had no place in the modern Elizabethan age.

Sleaze had also crept into the picture. A girl needed a sponsor to be presented, and sponsors had to be women who'd been presented themselves. It had become the practice for some of those ladies - now strapped for cash - to approach rich, social-climbing fathers and offer to present their daughters. For a suitable fee and expenses, of course!

MIXED-BAG OSCARS MEAN FROTH WINS OVER GRIT

I n a year which saw some pretty hard-hitting movies win nominations after scoring big at the box-office, the Academy of Motion Picture Arts and Sciences voters played it safe and gave the high-profile Oscars to films and performances which fell stolidly into the 'nice' category.

The grit was delivered in the shape of Best Picture nominations for Tennessee Williams' steamy sex drama *Cat On A Hot Tin Roof,* which also gave Paul Newman and Elizabeth Taylor well-deserved shortlistings as lead players, and *The Defiant Ones,* the mixed-race convict chase epic which earned Tony Curtis, Sidney Poitier and Theodore Bikel the chance to compete in the best and supporting actor contests.

Also providing muscle were the death-cell thriller *I Want To Live!,* with nominations for director Robert Wise and star Susan Hayward, and Spencer Tracy's solo *tour de force* in Ernest Hemingway's *The Old Man And The Sea.*

The froth came in the pretty pastel shades of the eventually-victorious Best Picture *Gigi,* which also provided an Oscar win for director Vincent Minnelli, though winsome star Leslie Caron mysteriously failed to be nominated, and the musical *Auntie Mame,* for which leading lady Rosalind Russell was entered for the Best Actress trophy.

In the event, having given *Gigi* the two main creative prizes, the Academy also passed on the chance to give the Best Actor award to men who'd made brave artistic statements and gave it to the very English David Niven, playing in the very *English Separate Tables.* Justice, of sorts, came in Susan Hayward's Best Actress trophy.

All in all, *Gigi* did very well, also winning Alan Jay Lerner two Oscars (one for Adapted Screenplay, the other as co-writer, with Frederick Loewe, of the title song), a Colour Cinematography award for Joseph Ruttenberg, one for editor Adrienne Fazan, and others for Andre Previn (Best Score), William Horning and Preston Ames (Art Direction) and Cecil Beaton (Costume Design).

Oh yes - Maurice Chevalier coincidentally won an Honorary Oscar. Ah, yes, I remember it well!

Hotly-tipped to win heaps, but eventually scoring pretty well null points, the musical *South Pacific* only scraped in with one nomination/win, for Best Sound.

Paul Newman and Elizabeth Taylor in
Tennessee William's steamy drama Cat
On A Hot Tin Roof

APRIL

Arnie Wins His First US Masters

Arnold Palmer took his first step into the big-time history books today in Augusta, Georgia when he won his first US Masters title. Only two years after winning the US Amateur and deciding to make golf his career, the 28 year old beat Fred Hawkins and Doug Ford by a stroke to gain the honour of donning the distinctive green champion's blazer for the first of three occasions - he would also take the title in 1960 and 1962.

Among the other victories which would make Palmer one of golf's most successful practitioners through the sixties and early seventies were the US Open (in 1960), the British Open (in 1961 and '62), the Australian and Spanish Opens and the British PGA. He would also captain America's Ryder Cup team and enjoy four seasons as the world's biggest earner.

12,000 CND Protestors Rally At British Nuclear HQ

A CROWD OF 12,000 SUPPORTERS of Britain's new Campaign for Nuclear Disarmament (CND) movement descended on the UK's H-bomb HQ - the Atomic Weapons Research Establishment at Aldermaston, Berkshire - today for a protest rally which called on Britain, the United States and Soviet Russia to end the manufacture, testing and storage of atomic weapons.

Entertained by a jazz band playing trad standards like When The Saints Go Marching In, the rally was a triumphant finale to a three-day march, from London to the sleepy town some 50 miles west, by a hard core of more than 600 CND activists whose ranks had swelled to 3,000 during the last leg. They led the march to the AWRE's barbed wire perimeter fence, accompanied by a relatively small detachment of police.

They weren't needed. Apart from a brief flurry when walkers charged a car which broadcast loudspeaker taunts that they were 'playing Khrushchev's game', the rally mood was described as friendly and relaxed, with bearded students and brightly dressed girls marching alongside pram-pushing parents and earnest academics.

Main speakers at the rally were the American pacifist Beyard Rustin, leading liberal German churchman Pastor Niemöller, and Stuart Morris of the British-based Peace Pledge Union. If world leaders pay no heed to CND's message, the organizers have said they will repeat the march next Easter - and every year until the world's nuclear arsenals are dismantled.

Eisenhower Calls For Civilian-Run Space Team

With everyone only too aware that the United States had been caught on the hop by the USSR's early leading burst in the space race while America had managed only one long-delayed satellite launch and more exploded rockets than flights, a clearly concerned President Eisenhower called for a civilian-controlled space agency in Washington today.

Until now, all US endeavours had been planned and managed by military personnel headed by Werner von Braun, now director of the US Ballistic Missile Agency in Alabama, but one-time head of the Nazis' V-2 programme which fired more than a thousand rockets at England during the last six months of WWII.

It was known that a number of eminent physicists, chemists and technical aces were reluctant to apply their much-needed skills to a military enterprise, so it was only good sense to make the space project a civilian operation.

Ike's dream would be realized on July 29 with the official creation of NASA - the National Aeronautical and Space Administration. Its director? Dr Werner von Braun.

APRIL 30

London Critics Rave Over Julie's 'Luverly' Fair Lady

A SMASH HIT FOR the past two years on Broadway, the musical *My Fair Lady* finally opened in London's Drury Lane Theatre tonight to universal acclaim from the ranks of critics who joined a glittering crowd of celebrities to see Julie Andrews and Rex Harrison reprise the roles which made them America's hottest ticket.

The show, written by Alan J Lerner and Frederick Loewe, was based on George Bernard Shaw's play *Pygmalion,* which depicted the transformation of Eliza Doolittle, a cockney flower seller, into a socially-acceptable 'lady' by Henry Higgins, a crusty professor of phonetics. Everything about the evening was given rave notices: the songs, which included the already well-known *Wouldn't It Be Luverly, On The Street Where You Live, Get Me To The Church On Time* and *The Rain In Spain* Julie Andrews' feisty but vulnerable Eliza, Harrison's insufferably superior but flawed Higgins, and the Cecil Beaton stage sets - especially the lush Ascot Racecourse scene - which were a beautiful re-creation of Edwardian life and style.

The reviews were a special triumph for Julie Andrews. A radio child star in the late forties, she'd risked a lot to quit Britain and seek her fame and fortune in the tough world of New York theatreland. Tonight proved there were no hard feelings as London welcomed back its own with a standing ovation and enough bouquets to keep Eliza in business for life.

Hollywood Transfixed By Turner Murder

Hollywood thrives on scandal and gossip, and there was plenty of both to fascinate and appal in the saga which broke tonight with the arrest of Oscar-nominated actress Lana Turner (pictured with daughter Cheryl), after the fatal stabbing of her gangster lover, Johnny Stompanato.

Stompanato's death came only days after he'd beaten Turner up when she returned from the Academy Awards ceremony, where she'd failed to win the Best Actress Oscar for her hit movie Peyton Place. He was angry that she'd refused to take him. The scandal intensified when, only hours after the news broke, it was learned that it was actually Turner's 14 year old daughter, Cheryl, who'd been charged with murder.

When the televised hearings got under way, millions of viewers were treated to a feast of sleaze, brutality, hints of Mafia connections, and a full description of how Cheryl Turner had run a long-bladed kitchen knife through Stompanato's body to save her mother from further abuse when he'd threatened to scar her for life.

The jury believed her story, and Cheryl was acquitted on the grounds of justifiable homicide. Her mother was given an amazing $2 million for her next movie, Imitation Of Life, while a re-released Peyton Place became a box office hit all over again.

Belgian King Opens World Fair

With all due pomp and ceremony, King Baudouin of Belgium performed the official opening ceremony of the World Fair in Brussels today.

The Fair, a high-tech celebration of international achievement in the fields of art, technology, science and modern post-war progress, was also a design and planning triumph for the Belgian capital. Set in a newly-created park and dominated by a vast futuristic sci-fi sphere, the site would remain as a valuable asset once the Fair ended its scheduled three-month run.

US Drops Treason Charges Against Poet Pound

Ezra Pound - the controversial American-born poet who made pro-Mussolini, anti-US and anti-Semitic broadcasts during WWII and had been held in an insane asylum since his arrest by American troops in 1945 - was today told that the treason charges he'd faced for the past 13 years had been dropped. Now aged 73, he was free to return to Italy, where he would die in 1972, his artistic reputation regained.

Born in Idaho, Pound moved to Europe in 1908, living in Venice, London and Paris before returning to Italy in 1924, where his A Draft Of XVI Cantos - part of an epic series of poems which dominated his working life - attracted the admiration and patronage of Italian dictator Benito Mussolini.

No Fairy-Tale Final For Busby's Babes

There was no Boys' Own comic book victory for Manchester United, the team of young soccer giants created by Matt Busby which - despite the horrendous crash which wiped out eight of their brightest talents in February - managed to reach today's FA Cup Final at Wembley Stadium, their second successive appearance in the competition.

Going into the game with the emotional good wishes of all Britain's neutral soccer fans, the hastily patched-together Busby Babes met an in-form Bolton Wanderers who, while they were undoubtedly as sympathetic as any to United's tragedy, weren't going to let that sympathy stand in the way of making the most of their chance to collect coveted winners' medals and put the FA Cup in their club trophy cabinet.

Bolton duly emerged as 2-0 victors in a game which, while not memorable for action, memorably reinforced the terrible loss Manchester United and British soccer had suffered in Munich on February 6.

Scandal: Wild Rocker Jerry Lee Flees London With Child Bride

ROCK 'N' ROLL MUSIC PRODUCED its first major scandal today when Jerry Lee Lewis (pictured), the piano-thumping self-proclaimed wild man of rock, was forced to cancel a scheduled five week tour of Britain and return to America with the 13 year old girl London newspapers had revealed was his wife. Audiences at the three shows he had played were openly hostile, shouting abuse and throwing objects as the 24 year old tried to perform.

A media storm erupted when Lewis, who had enjoyed a string of huge international hits with frantic songs like *Whole Lotta Shakin' Goin' On, Great Balls Of Fire,* and the ironically-apt *High School Confidential,* casually mentioned to a journalist that the young Myra, who was his third wife, was indeed only 13, and was also his cousin. He omitted to mention that he'd married her before his last marriage had been legally annulled!

Although marriage to a 13 year old may have been legally acceptable in Jerry Lee's home state of Louisiana, and his adopted base in Memphis, Tennessee, British press and public clearly found it morally reprehensible and the former Bible University student was hounded out of the country.

How wild was Jerry Lee? On one occasion, the man known as 'The Killer' was forced to perform on stage before Chuck Berry. At the end of his barnstorming set he poured petrol into the piano and threw in a lighted match. Strolling through the smoke past an open-mouthed Berry, Lewis drawled: 'Follow that!'

Dungeness Chosen As Next Nuclear Plant Site

Dungeness, situated on one of the most desolate stretches of the Kent coastline, was named as the site for Britain's fifth nuclear power station today in London.

The decision to build the latest of an eventual 12 nuclear plants, which were originally scheduled to cost around £300 million ($900m), at Dungeness was good news for the local economy but bad news for opponents of a technology many believe is too dangerous and unpredictable. Despite protests, the Central Electricity Generating Board's newest and most expensive 'baby' would go ahead, joining the conventional power station at Dungeness.

Ike Rejects Nuclear-Free Europe Plan

A brief vision of a Europe free of atomic weapons faded instantly today in Washington when President Eisenhower rejected a Polish government proposal that the continent's growing arsenal of nuclear missiles should be dismantled.

The proposal, made at recent talks by senior government officials, is believed to have been rejected not because it came from the Poles, but because White House experts were certain the idea had been planted on Russian orders and the Soviets were not to be trusted.

UK TOP 10 SINGLES

1: Who's Sorry Now
- Connie Francis
2: Whole Lotta Woman
- Marvin Rainwater
3: A Wonderful Time Up There
- Pat Boone
4: Tom Hark
- Elias & His Zig Zag Flutes
5: Wear My Ring Around Your Neck
- Elvis Presley
6: Lollipop
- The Mudlarks
7: Grand Coolie Dam
- Lonnie Donegan
8: Swingin' Shepherd Blues
- Ted Heath Orchestra
9: Lollipop
- The Chordettes
10: Breathless
- Jerry Lee Lewis

MAY 13

Algeria: Civil War Looms As French Nationalists Rebel

THE WAR OF WORDS OVER Algerian independence, which has divided France for the past two years, threatened to throw the country into a full-blown civil war today when a 40,000-strong mob of French settlers took matters into their own hands, stormed and seized government buildings in Algiers and set up an *ad hoc* government they called The Committee of Public Safety.

In Paris, the government of Prime Minister Pierre Pflimlin acted to prevent the conflict spreading to Metropolitan France, sealing the north African territory off by banning all journeys by 'unofficial persons' to and from Algeria and ordering the arrest of 80 right-wing extremists likely to orchestrate support for the settlers, offensively nicknamed '*les pieds-noir*'.

While crowds of police, troops, settlers and students surrounded the Ministry of Algeria which the Committee of Safety had captured as their HQ, the French military commander, General Salan, broadcast an emotional message confirming that he had taken the destiny of French Algeria into his own hands. 'I ask you to put your trust in the army and show your trust and determination', he said.

A similar call was made from Algiers Radio, which had been over-run by rebel paratroops. Admitting that they still awaited news from Paris, a Committee member said they had reason to believe the battle was won. 'Algeria will remain French forever', he proclaimed defiantly.

Although Pflimlin would send army chief General Henri Lorillot to Algiers on May 21 in a bid to negotiate a compromise peace settlement, the situation remained poised on the edge of a perilous precipice.

MAY 23

Cockerell's Craft Hovers Into History

Unveiled to British marine journalists today, the new invention of Suffolk boatbuilder Christopher Cockerell excited the imaginations of those who can see the potential of the vehicle he has called The Hovercraft.

Capable of travelling over land and water without any change to controls or physical status, the Hovercraft floats on a cushion of air generated by a relatively-modest fan. Jets of air directed inwards from the edge of a galvanized rubber 'skirt' help maintain the supporting pressure which lifts the machine.

The government-backed National Research and Development Organisation was reported to be taking a keen interest in Cockerell's craft, which offered a wide range of possible uses, from flexible passenger-carrying to versatile military transportation of troops and supplies across varied terrain.

De Gaulle Returns To Solve Algerian Crisis

MAY 29

A political exile for the past 12 years, France's wartime hero and former president, Charles de Gaulle, returned triumphantly to the centre of the national stage today when he agreed to accept the post of Prime Minister and the task of trying to solve the increasingly-volatile Algerian crisis. He is to be sworn in on June 1.

The General, who resigned as President of a provisional post-war government in 1946 over the constitution of the new 4th Republic, returned only under the strict condition that he would have full powers for 'a determined period' with a mandate to re-write the French constitution. The National Assembly had no option but to accept de Gaulle's terms. Public opinion in France and Algeria

overwhelmingly told them that the powerful charisma of the former Free French commander made him the only man likely to be able to stop France tearing itself apart. News of the general's return was the signal for thousands to gather at the National Assembly chanting 'de Gaulle to power!' and Paris was filled with cars sounding their horns in rhythm with the chant.

JUNE 25

Lebanese Ask US To Halt UAR Arms Flow

The embattled Lebanese government, trying to stem a constant challenge to its authority from Muslim guerrillas, today appealed to the US government to halt the flow of arms and explosives it claimed were being supplied by the Egyptian-led United Arab Republic.

While the United States is heavily represented in the region by the US 6th Fleet, it is not clear what actions it could take to make any difference. Few, if any, of the supplies reaching the Lebanese rebels arrived by sea and there was nothing American forces could do to block the movement of arms from the land-locked Syria, co-founder of the UAR.

Political stability in Lebanon had been a fragile flower since the creation of a compromise constitution in 1944. This gave the presidency to a succession of Maronite Christians, the prime ministership to Sunni Muslims and the role of speaker in the parliament to a fundamentalist Shia Muslim. It also created an atmosphere of intense rivalry for real power.

JUNE 20

Cyprus Curfew Ordered As Makarios Rejects Peace Plan

An island-wide curfew was ordered by British authorities in Cyprus today as Archbishop Makarios, the exiled Greek Cypriot leader, rejected a new peace plan intended to avoid a fresh outbreak of warfare between the Mediterranean colony's Turkish and Greek communities. Only 12 days earlier, four people had died and more than 70 had been injured in riots.

The Archbishop, resident in the Greek capital Athens since his release from an enforced exile in the Seychelles in April last year, turned down a suggested seven-year period of continued British rule and control of internal security while a system of autonomous government was devised by the two Cyprus communities.

The Greek community is apparently not prepared to compromise its aim to forge official political links with mainland Greece and gain full independence from Britain. Its fight would continue to be led by the terrorist activities of EOKA, the guerrilla organization led by Colonel George Grivas. The Turks, for their part, continued to seek political parity with the Greeks, even though they were outnumbered four to one.

French Rebels Dismayed By De Gaulle's Equal Rights Message

ANY HOPES REBELLIOUS French settlers may have held that Charles de Gaulle's return signalled victory for their bid to keep Algeria French were dashed in Algiers today when he told a vast crowd of *'pieds noir'* who'd come to hear him speak from the balcony of Government House, that the country's Arab nationalists were due full civil rights.

Brought back to power only three days earlier by those who shared the aims of the thousands who cheered his appearance on the balcony, the general began with words which led them to believe he approved of their actions last month.

'I have understood you', de Gaulle told them. 'I know what has happened here. I see what you have wanted to do. I see that the road that you have opened in Algeria is that of renovation and of brotherhood.'

Knowing that fraternity and renewal were not their objectives, the crowd grew increasingly nervous and restive, a mood which worsened the longer de Gaulle spoke. By the time he conceded that the Algerian nationalists were courageous fighters and he accepted equal rights and integration for men and women, Europeans and Moslem alike, the crowd was clearly anxious.

De Gaulle's final remarks did nothing to lessen the confusion and tension. 'There are only Frenchmen, Frenchmen with full citizenship and the same obligations', he insisted.

With a clear hint at an offer of amnesty for Arab rebels, the general concluded: 'To these men, I, de Gaulle, open the door of reconciliation.'

UK TOP 10 SINGLES

1: Who's Sorry Now
- Connie Francis
2: On The Street Where You Live
- Vic Damone
3: Tom Hark
- Elias & His Zig Zag Flutes
4: Stairway Of Love
- Michael Holliday
5: You Need Hands/Tulips From Amsterdam
- Max Bygraves
6: All I Have To Do Is Dream/Claudette
- The Everly Brothers
7: Witch Doctor
- Don Lang
8: A Wonderful Time Up There
- Pat Boone
9: The Army Game
- TV Cast
10: Lollipop
- The Mudlarks

ARRIVALS

Born this month:

7: Prince (Prince Rogers Nelson), US superstar musician, writer, arranger, producer, actor

11: Hugo Sanchez, Mexican international soccer star

13: Peter Scudamore, British National Hunt jockey, record 1678 career wins, retired 1993

15: Wade Boggs, US baseball star, Boston Red Sox (1982-92), NY Yankees, All-Star team 1993; Neil Arthur, UK pop musician (Blancmange)

29: Rosa Mota, Portuguese Olympic gold (1988) and World marathon queen

DEPARTURES

Died this month:

9: Friedrich Robert Donat, British Oscar-winning film and stage actor (*Goodbye Mr Chips, The Winslow Boy, The Ghost Goes West, etc*)

16: Imre Nagy, Hungarian statesman (*see main story*)

18: Douglas Jardine, English international cricketer

JUNE 29

Brazil Baffle Sweden To Win Soccer World Cup

Brazil, long the most admired and feared footballing nation in the world, but let down in previous tournaments by a mixture of tantrums and ill-discipline in crucial games, won the World Cup at last today when, with a dazzling display of skills, they beat their Swedish hosts 5-2 in Stockholm.

Brightest new star of a stellar Brazilian team was 17 year old Pele, who scored two goals in the course of giving Sweden - and the watching world - a thrilling lesson in ball control, inventive fast-thinking and poise.

(For the full World Cup story, see Sports pages)

England Teens Rock As Oh Boy! Hits TV Screens

Positive reaction to two test broadcasts this month have convinced the British independent ABC-TV to go ahead with a whole series of *Oh Boy!*, a fast-moving rock music extravaganza devised and produced by Jack Good, the man who created *Six-Five Special* for BBC Television last year. His new show will begin a 13-week run in September.

While the BBC show would remain hugely popular, its relatively-small studio setting and the cosy presentation style of hosts Pete Murray and Josephine Douglas would be quickly overtaken by the big, brash and breakneck style of *Oh Boy!*

Packing 17 songs into its hectic, unlinked 35 minutes, the *Oh Boy!* pilots were built around a nucleus of new British heart-throb Marty Wilde (pictured), The Dallas Boys, South African rock organist Cherry Wainer and a big house band imaginatively called Lord Rockingham's XI.

Just before it was officially launched, the *Oh Boy!* cast of regulars would be enlarged by the addition of Cliff Richard. Originally hyped as Britain's answer to Elvis Presley, he was destined to become one of the most successful international artists the country has ever produced.

JUNE 1

Alfie Does Runner Number Three

He may not have been much good at stealing - something which he denied having done anyway - but Alfie Hinds proved he had every right to the 'British Houdini' title he'd been given by the press when he escaped from Chelmsford Prison today.

It was Hinds' third successful self-liberation in little more than a year and was achieved by the simple ploy of climbing a 20-feet wall to make his break. A red-faced Home Office spokesman confirmed that Hinds, who used the inevitable front page coverage of his escapes to protest his innocence, would be moved to an even more secure prison if - and when - he was recaptured.

Hungarian Regime Hangs Uprising Hero Nagy

THE RUSSIAN PUPPET REGIME of Hungarian Prime Minister János Kádár outraged world opinion today when it announced the execution of Imre Nagy, the premier whose liberal reforms and decision to quit the Warsaw Pact in 1956 led to the anti-Soviet uprising which Russian tanks crushed in a few brief days of horrific brutality.

Typical of reaction was the US statement released in Washington the next day - President Eisenhower described Nagy's hanging as 'a shocking act of cruelty'. On June 23, official protests from the communist Yugoslav and Polish governments would be handed to Hungarian Foreign Office officials.

Driven to seek refuge in the Yugoslavian Embassy in Budapest when the Soviet Army invaded Hungary, Nagy had remained there for 18 days before agreeing to surrender to the secret police force of his Russian-appointed successor, Kádár - a man he'd believed had shared his dream of a neutral Hungary, and the person who personally guaranteed Nagy's safety if he left the embassy.

That promise proved hollow. It is now known that Nagy - along with a number of other leaders of the doomed uprising - had shared the same fate of a secret trial followed by hanging.

MAGNIFICENT MICKEY MOVES TO LIFT WOMEN'S GOLF

Her parents may have named her Kathryn, but everyone knew her as Mickey Wright, the supreme golf stylist whose victory in this year's US Women's Open and the LPGA Championship marked the arrival of a player destined to elevate women's professional golf in public esteem more than perhaps any other except the extrovert Babe Zaharias.

Born in San Diego, California, the daughter of a lawyer who encouraged her sporting ambitions as soon as she had them, Mickey was playing golf by the age of 11, and had won the Southern California Girls' title two years later.

A shy and retiring character, Mickey became US Girls' Champion in 1952, aged only 17 and beating the likes of Barbara McIntire, Anne Quast, Judy Bell and Margaret Smith. In the 1954 Women's Open her fourth place also made her top amateur. And while she lost 4 & 2 in the final of the National Amateur later in the same year, Mickey decided to turn pro.

Spending the first year polishing her game by playing and learning from watching major players like Louise Suggs, Betty Jameson, Zaharias and Patty Berg, Mickey won the Jacksonville Open just 16 months after turning pro, won three more in 1957, and this year did what no other woman had when she took the Open and the LPGA.

No other woman had achieved her feat of retaining the Open in 1959, and her eventual 82 major victories, which would include four Opens and four LPGAs, included a spell in 1962 when the name Mickey Wright was on all four US major trophies - the Open, LPGA, the Titleholders and the Western Women's Open - at the same time.

Ben Hogan once said that Mickey Wright had the best swing he ever saw from a man or woman. Countless thousands of women saw that swing and decided to give it a go. When she first started to play professionally, the total prize money on offer was $135,000. By the time she finally called it a day, in 1979, there was a total of $4,400,000 available.

REAL MAKE IT THREE IN A ROW

Real Madrid kept their remarkable unbeaten record in the European Cup this year when they beat Italian champions Milan 3-2 in the final, held in Brussels in front of a mind-boggled 67,000 fans - so keeping the title they won at the inaugural Paris final in 1956 when they beat Stade de Reims 4-3, and held on to last year by beating Fiorentina 2-0 in their Madrid stadium.

Nobody present could have suspected that Real would go on to win the next two finals as well, to set a five-win record unlikely ever to be beaten, but they were aware that in skipper Alfredo DiStefano they were seeing a master at work. Maintaining his own personal achievement of scoring in every final, he duly made it on to the scoresheet alongside Hector Rial and Paco Gento, while Milan could only manage goals from Grillo and Schiaffino in reply.

Missing from the night, of course, were the Manchester United team so hotly tipped to be finalists this year, but so cruelly mown down in the Munich air crash. The survivors of Matt Busby's 'Babes' had to be content with a second successive defeat in the FA Cup at Wembley as an unsatisfactory end to a horribly tragic season.

RECORDS TUMBLE AS DERBYSHIRE MASSACRE HANTS

August 14, 1958 has gone down in English country cricketing history for reasons supporters of Hampshire will not want recounted. But the simple fact is, in a remarkable day's cricket at Burton-on-Trent a total of 39 wickets fell in a match which saw Hampshire's two joint top scorers in the first innings manage only five runs each, with the biggest stand being only six.

Having skittled Derbyshire out for a first-innings total of only 74, with Heath's bowling figures 6-35 and Shackleton's 4-36, Hampshire could have anticipated an easy stroll to a hefty lead. Instead, they faced only 16.4 overs of Jackson and Rhodes' bowling and were all out for 23 - Jackson turning in 5-10 and Rhodes 4-12 to humiliate the visitors.

Worse was to come. Derbyshire managed to scramble 107 runs in their second innings, giving a stunned Hampshire a win target of 159, surely attainable if everyone kept their heads. The only problem was, Jackson and Rhodes kept theirs too, and Hampshire were bowled out for a mere 55. On that occasion Jackson's wicket tally was 5-10 and Rhodes' was 4-12.

It was not until 6.40 pm that Derbyshire introduced a third bowler, Morgan. He didn't need to warm up and promptly took three Hampshire wickets for only four runs in 5.3 overs. The massacre was complete. The mighty were humbled.

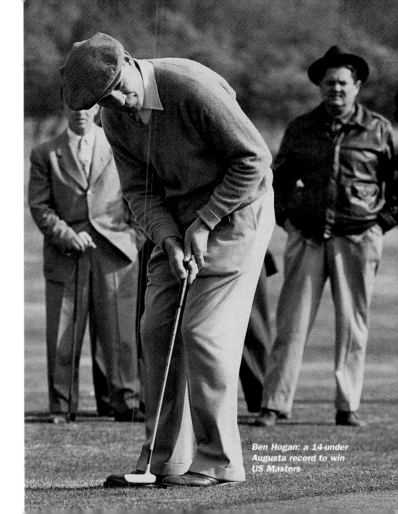

Ben Hogan: a 14-under Augusta record to win US Masters

JULY 14

East And West Lock Horns As Middle East Explodes

TENSIONS BOILED OVER INTO CRISIS this month in the Middle East, beginning with the assassination of the pro-Western 23 year old King Faisal of Iraq and his uncle, Crown Prince Abdulillah, by army officers inspired by Egypt's President Nasser, and ending with the arrival of US Marines in the Lebanese capital Beirut and British paratroops flying in to the Jordanian capital Amman. The Soviet Union used events to rattle a sabre in the United Nations and offer 'volunteers' to Nasser.

The fuse was lit in the Iraqi capital, Baghdad, on July 14 when a group of young officers murdered the young King Faisal and his powerful uncle. Supporters of the coup captured the prime minister, General Nuri el-Said, who was kicked to death by a street mob.

Jordan - Iraq's partner in the recently-formed Arab Union, the pro-Western rival to President Nasser's nationalist United Arab Republic - was inevitably and immediately drawn into the crisis. So was Lebanon, whose President Camille Chamoun was already fighting UAR-funded rebels. It was Chamoun who issued a call for US assistance.

That call was answered on July 15 when 1,700 marines of the US 6th Fleet waded ashore at Beirut, to be greeted by bikini-clad Lebanese sunseekers offering ice cream to the combat equipment-laden Americans - probably the easiest amphibious landing in modern warfare.

On July 17, 2,000 British paras flew into Amman in RAF Hastings and Beverly transport planes in response to King Hussein's request for help in confronting the Syrian UAR troops which Jordan's UN ambassador reported massing on the border.

Enraged at US and UK intervention, the Soviets demanded that the UN order their troops out of the region. Their call was countered by America's representative, Henry Cabot Lodge, who said that 'if the United Nations cannot deal with indirect aggression, the United Nations will break up'.

In London, Labour opposition to British involvement was expressed in parliamentary speeches by leader Hugh Gaitskell and left-winger Aneurin Bevan, who said the UK should avoid collision with Russia at all costs. A crucial vote supporting Prime Minister Harold Macmillan was carried by a government majority of sixty-three.

In Jordan, meanwhile, King Hussein broke off diplomatic relations with the UAR in response to their involvement in the Iraqi coup. British troops were flown from Kenya to the Persian Gulf port of Bahrein to head off potential unrest there, with other units arriving in Malta and Cyprus in case reinforcements were needed in Jordan.

As the US concentrated 44 warships off the Lebanese coast, the Soviets announced that large-scale 'manoeuvres' were being held close to the USSR's Turkish and Persian borders. A great Mexican stand-off had begun.

Cyprus Reels As Death Toll Mounts

The failure of last month's British peace proposals appear to have sparked off even greater and more horrific terrorist action in Cyprus this month. Almost 40 people - civilians from both the Greek and Turkish communities, as well as British servicemen - were killed in two spells of concentrated violence.

A six-day spell of bombing and gun attacks by the EOKA guerrillas of Greek Cypriot leader General George Grivas ended on July 13 with official sources confirming that 31 had died.

On July 31, eight more died in a one-day outbreak of renewed action aimed at Turkish targets, British military and civilian vehicles and businesses known to work for UK organizations.

UK TOP 10 SINGLES

1: All I Have To Do Is Dream/Claudette
- The Everly Brothers

2: On The Street Where You Live
- Vic Damone

3: You Need Hands/Tulips From Amsterdam
- Max Bygraves

4: Big Man
- The Four Preps

5: Twilight Time
- The Platters

6: Who's Sorry Now
- Connie Francis

7: Sugar Moon
- Pat Boone

8: Book Of Love
- The Mudlarks

9: Rave On
- Buddy Holly

10: Witch Doctor
- Don Lang

JULY 5

Thomson Triumph Makes It Four British Opens In Past Five

When you're hot, you're hot. If anyone needed proof that Australia's Peter Thomson was the most consistent and (don't tell the Americans!) best golfer in the world right now, his victory today in the British Open at Lytham St Anne's must have settled any arguments.

Taking the Open for the fourth time in his past five appearances, Thomson hammered home his superiority by achieving the feat with a record 63 in the last-round play-off against Britain's David Thomas. That said, it was his hardest-won championship of all. The 23 year old Sudbury pro had won a 36-hole stroke-play decider against Thomson by beating Scotland's Eric Brown and Irishman Christy O'Connor by one stroke to match Thomson's 278. The play-off was tight and thrilling, but Thomson's nerve held - he won by four clear strokes to enter the record books.

JULY 31

Death Toll Mounts As Tibetans Hit Chinese Army

REPORTS REACHING THE OUTSIDE world today from the Himalayan country of Tibet suggest that local resistance to the eight-year Chinese occupation had intensified in recent months. With a daily death toll of around 300, it was estimated that 15,000 Tibetans and up to 50,000 Chinese had been killed in fighting between troops of the puppet regime in the capital, Lhasa, and guerrillas based in the remote mountainous region of eastern Tibet.

More than 150,000 rebels were involved in attacks which had seen the destruction of strategic bridges and roads to isolate Chinese garrisons and limit their access to supplies, except by air-drops. Chinese morale is said to be very low.

Tibetan resistance is being masterminded by a group of leading exiles based in India, which has refused to recognize their struggle because it would bring India into conflict with China.

As Tibetan government officials in Lhasa - one-time supporters of the country's spiritual leader, the Dalai Lama - are said to be actively collaborating with the Chinese, the exiles warned that the situation was moving beyond settlement by peaceful means.

JULY 26

Charles Is Created Prince Of Wales

Queen Elizabeth maintained six hundred years of tradition today when a Buckingham Palace statement announced that Prince Charles, heir to the British throne, had been created Prince of Wales.

It has long been customary for male heirs to the throne to be created Prince of Wales, a title which dates from a time when the United Kingdom was a less robust union and future kings were actually based for long periods of time in what was still a rebellious outpost of the expanded realm. It will be left to the young prince to decide how direct and how strong his links with Wales will be. In the event, he would spend part of his college years as a student at Aberystwyth University and take a very active role in local affairs to prove his new title was not merely honorific.

JULY 31

Papa Doc To Rule Haiti

François 'Papa Doc' Duvalier became the virtual dictator of Haiti today when the Caribbean island's Congress granted his request to rule by decree for six months, allowing him to mop up the last vestiges of an army rebellion his regime crushed with the help of a core of loyal officers and the presidential palace guard. The coup attempt began when a 100-man rebel force over-ran and occupied an army barracks opposite Duvalier's palace in the capital, Port-au-Prince. Attacked by troops loyal to the president, the rebels were defeated in a hard gun battle.

Rebel morale sank when it was learned that Louis Dejoie and Paul Magloire, the exiled leaders of the rebellion, had been tracked down and executed by two army captains.

JULY 10

Parking Meters Given London Trial Run

Mayfair, London's swishest shopping centre, today became the unwilling guinea pig in an experiment of the newest thing calculated to drive the capital's motorists mad - parking meters.

Police reported that while traffic moved more smoothly in affected streets, drivers were noticeably wary of the new-fangled machines and many spaces were left vacant all day. They also admitted that many car owners simply drove away from metered streets to find space in those not yet cursed.

There also seemed to be confusion about the rules of the game, with some people complaining that refunds were not available for unused time and commercial drivers saying they were forced to pay most because they couldn't be sure how long their visits to customers would actually last.

AUG

New York Ticker-Tape Welcome For North Pole Sub Heroes

NEW YORK REFLECTED America's pride in a breathtaking achievement today when it staged a traditional ticker-tape welcome for the officers and crew of *Nautilus*, the atomic submarine which recently completed the first-ever undersea voyage beneath the ice cap which covers the North Pole.

The sub's epic journey began from Hawaii's Pearl Harbor on August 23 on a heading which took her north through the Bering Strait between Alaska and Russia. *Nautilus* dived under the Polar ice cap off Alaska and continued her course under the North Pole - a trip which took four days, broken only by one stop to force the periscope through the ice to check bearings.

Every member of the *Nautilus* crew - who ended their historic voyage at Iceland on August 27 - received a citation to honour their achievement, with her skipper, Commander WR Anderson, being awarded the Legion of Merit medal.

The security, strategic and trade implications of the *Nautilus* crossing were quickly picked up by commentators on both sides of the Iron Curtain. Western military experts said it could open the Arctic for submarine-originated missile attacks - something Soviet sources were quick to cite as proof of the United States' aggressive intentions.

More fanciful, perhaps, was the seriously-made suggestion that *Nautilus* had also opened the way for a fleet of cargo-carrying submarines which could use the trans-Polar route to speed deliveries between Europe, the American west coast and a number of Pacific nations.

Britain Hit By Youth And Race Riots

The month ended with two nights of street violence in Britain which had very different causes but similar terrible implications for the immediate future.

On August 30, Nottingham police moved in on the city centre to break up a gathering of 500 Teddy Boys, the rock 'n' roll fraternity whose increased presence on British streets had begun calls for greater control. By the end of a series of running battles, 36 people had been arrested and charged with violence, resisting arrest and causing damage to city stores and pubs.

The other unrest was the most disturbing evidence yet that many British nationals harboured deep racial hatred for the rising number of black immigrants - mostly from the West Indies - who'd made their homes in British cities during the past eight years, their emigration encouraged by successive governments.

On August 30, gangs of white youths began invading the largely black west London area of Notting Hill. Hurling bricks, bottles and racial taunts at innocent residents, they were met with resistance which ended with a concerted police action and arrest - on the second night of violence - of 13 people.

ARRIVALS

Born this month:
4: Greg Foster, US Olympic and World 100m hurdles champion
7: Bruce Dickinson, UK rock singer (Iron Maiden), international fencing champion, DJ
13: Feargal Sharkey, Irish rock singer (The Undertones)
16: Madonna (Madonna Louise Ciccone), US singer, dancer, actress, pornographer
17: Belinda Carlisle, US pop singer
29: Michael Jackson, superstar singer, dancer,writer,producer *(see Came & Went pages)*; Lenny Henry, UK comedian, writer, actor
31: Serge Blanco, French international rugby play-maker supremo, world's most capped player (93)

DEPARTURES

Died this month:
5: Joseph Holbrooke, composer
26: Ralph Vaughan Williams, British composer

AUGUST 28

Britain Prepares For Fish War

With less than a week to go before Iceland's recently-declared introduction of a new 12-mile fishing limit was due to come into force, a sizeable fleet of British trawlers arrived off the coast of Iceland today to begin work off the existing four-mile zone. The move caused an immediate breakdown in talks between the two countries which were being held at NATO headquarters in Paris, with a fishing war an increasing possibility.

As the Icelandic government in Reykjavik stood firmly by it's unilateral imposition of a 12-mile limit and said it would not sit at a conference table as long as Iceland was physically threatened, Royal Navy frigates were reported to be accompanying a second wave of British trawlers headed for Iceland.

Mono The Casualty As New Stereo Rules Radio Show

THERE MAY HAVE BEEN a few poor benighted souls out there who still relied on old wind-up gramophones, a pile of battered 78 rpm records and a dwindling supply of replaceable steel needles as their main source of home entertainment, but even those who'd made the move up-market and bought modern radiograms to combine record-playing and radio-listening became creatures of the Dark Ages today when London's annual Radio Show opened its doors.

It appeared that our lives were incomplete if we didn't have two loudspeakers, a record turntable and separate amplifier, along with yards of wiring, to play our fast-growing stack of 45 rpm singles and 33 rpm long-players.

High fidelity stereophonic sound systems were everywhere you looked, poised to boggle the ears and the imagination, create a whole new language replete with words like 'woofer', 'tweeter' and 'equalizer', and spell the death of boring old mono as the world's record companies caught up with those tape recorder manufact-urers who'd been selling two-track tape for years.

Arkansas Governor Ignores Supreme Court

Orval Faubus - the hard-line Governor of Arkansas whose early stand against President Eisenhower's determination to end racial segregation in southern state schools appeared to have crumbled last September, when Federal troops enforced the enrolment of black pupils in a Little Rock high school - proved that he considered Little Rock only a battle lost today when he refused to enforce a new Supreme Court order to integrate all Arkansas schools.

Last year the Governor, only one of a number of southern leaders either dragging their heels or staging belligerent rear-guard actions against attacks on white supremacy, was the named subject of actions brought to the Supreme Court by civil rights organizations angered by his continued refusal to meet the requirements of the President's legislation.

His renewed disobedience is bound to have serious repercussions in coming months, and the further intervention of Federal forces cannot be ruled out.

Superb Herb Smashes World Records

Herb Elliott, Australia's unbeatable mile supremo, had a huge crowd in Gothenburg, Sweden, on its feet today as he smashed his second world record in less than a month by demolishing the challenge of the Czech 1500 metre champion Stanislav Jungwirth and trimmed two seconds off his record of 3mins 38secs.

The 20 year old had set his first record of the month in Dublin, shortly after winning the 800m and mile gold medals at the Commonwealth Games in Cardiff. Running in an invitation mile, Elliott broke Derek Ibbotson's year-old record by two and a half seconds (reducing it to 3:57.2), finishing a full 15 yards ahead of the field.

Buddy And Buddies Make Double Assault On Stardom

It wasn't unusual for American rock 'n' roll acts to enjoy greater fame and far greater career longevity in Britain and Europe than they could enjoy or sustain at home. It wasn't simply a question of 'big fish in smaller ponds', though that was a factor. Now and again UK and European fans fell for an artist in a big way and stayed loyal and true long after the chart hits had dried - or the star himself died.

No case offers better proof than Buddy Holly, the Texas-born singer-songwriter who'd made his international chart breakthrough in August last year as lead singer with The Crickets. Their *That'll Be The Day*, a song written by Holly, Crickets drummer Jerry Allison and producer-manager Norman Petty had reached No.3 in the US and No.1 in Britain, to be followed by *Peggy Sue,* a single credited to Holly alone but actually featuring the same musician line-up billed as The Crickets.

By January this year the handy double-act ruse was working to perfection as both *Peggy Sue* (by Buddy Holly) and *Oh Boy!* (by The Crickets) nestled high in the American and British charts. By May The Crickets were back in the charts with *Maybe Baby,* with Buddy Holly's *Rave On* hitting in July and The Crickets' *Think It Over* charting in August.

A British concert tour consolidated Holly's star status so much that when he and the original Crickets went their separate ways and Holly abandoned the Clovis, New Mexico studios of Norman Petty and began recording solo in New York, the hits kept coming. The fact was, Buddy Holly wrote great songs and made great records, influencing a younger generation which included future Beatles bassist Paul McCartney, even inspiring the Crickets-like name for

the group he'd form with John Lennon.

Holly's death in a plane crash with fellow performers The Big Bopper and Ritchie Valens, in February 1959, would only solidify the loyalty of British and European fans. While he would largely become no more than a footnote and distant memory to the majority of American record-buyers, re-released, re-packaged or re-mixed recordings by the 22 year old would still feature in the British singles and albums charts for the next 30 years.

TV GIVES CLIFF INSTANT HIT

The launch of producer Jack Good's new *Oh Boy!* television series in Britain in September this year was to prove especially memorable for one of the show's regulars, newcomer Cliff Richard. An instant hit with the studio audience and viewers alike when *Oh Boy!* reached UK living rooms, the handsome 18 year old (billed as 'Britain's Elvis Presley', of course!), had the pleasure of seeing *Move It,* his debut single, race up the UK charts within days of release, making its first appearance at No.5.

Born Harry Webb, in Lucknow, India, Cliff had been spotted drawing screams from regulars at the *Two I's* coffee bar, the London HQ of the British skiffle boom. Signed to a recording deal by Columbia Records label boss Norrie Paramor, Cliff was added to the *Oh Boy!* stable by Good when Cliff's agent sent him a test pressing of *Move It.*

Written by Ian Samwell, a member of Cliff's backing group The Drifters (who'd soon be forced to become The Shadows to avoid confusion with the American vocal group), *Move It* had been intended to be the B-side of *Schoolboy Crush,* Cliff's version of an American song.

Released two weeks after Cliff and The Drifters made their

first appearance on *Oh Boy!* it would prove only the first of an unprecendented and almost unbroken series of huge international hits which made Cliff Richard the most consistent and successful pop star Britain has ever produced, whether it be as record-maker, film actor or concert performer.

CONWAY'S A HIT, YOU TWIT!

What's in a name? To an aspiring American rock and pop singer called Harold Jenkins who didn't think his real name had the right ring to it, the answer was 'everything', and the solution was simple: using a pin, a blindfold and a map of the USA, he'd locate a new image for himself.

As luck would have it, the pin landed on Conway, Arkansas and Twitty, Texas. Could have been worse, though when *It's Only Make Believe* - the record which ended a two-year period of aimless knocking on the door marked 'Big Time' to become one of this year's biggest-selling singles - first appeared in Britain, it was greeted with hoots of laughter and lampooned by Peter Sellers as a brainless pop singer he called Twit Conway.

The 25 year old Mississippian would have the last laugh, of course. Continuing to enjoy a fruitful pop and teen-movie career in the US, in 1965 he began to switch direction to become one of the most successful, popular and richest country music entertainers of the seventies and eighties, owning the Twitty City theme park, where you could buy Twittyburgers. He would die, on tour, in 1993.

Cliff Richard

SEPT

Notting Hill Torn By Worsening Race Riots

LONDON HAD ITS FIRST TASTE of the appalling violence which racial prejudice can cause when the incidents which first gained public attention at the end of last month erupted into full-scale riots tonight, turning the streets of Notting Hill into a debris-filled battleground and filling local hospitals' emergency departments with casualties, some of them seriously injured.

During the riots, which began when gangs of white youths returned to the area armed with batons and petrol bombs, police advised all black residents to remain indoors. The trouble was sparked by a mob of white youths who besieged a house occupied by black people. They were answered with a shower of milk bottles and a petrol bomb, which exploded into the street. This was followed by a full counter-attack by a group of black men armed with iron bars, and while police were able to break that fight up, word and trouble spread like wildfire. A black couple were chased down a nearby street by a white mob yelling 'Let's get the blacks!', and three petrol bombs were hurled at a group of men leaving a local black club.

Although press, radio and TV journalists reported an even-handed approach by police at the height of the riots, local black leaders were quoted as saying they didn't think enough had been done to protect black people and property. They did, however, agree with a Special Branch source who said there was reason to believe that right-wing extremists were behind the initial attacks.

The next morning, 59 people were charged with assault, carrying illegal weapons and other offences, prompting a local magistrate to describe the night's events as 'disgraceful'. Six days later, nine white youths were each jailed for four years for attacks on black people.

Castro Begins His Promised Push To Oust Batista

Fidel Castro, the socialist guerrilla leader whose forces have mounted an unceasing and increasingly popular campaign against the corrupt, Mafia-backed Cuban regime of President Fulgencio Batista, today launched the major offensive he'd been promising for almost a year.

Six columns were reported to have left Castro's mountain stronghold in western Cuba, but as those reports emanated from a rebel radio station, government officials in the capital, Havana, felt able to dismiss them as empty propaganda. There is no doubt, however, that Batista's generals took them seriously enough to order a full mobilization of the Cuban army and air force. Two rebel columns were confirmed to be heading into the central province of Camaguey. One was led by Castro's brother, Raul. The other was commanded by an Argentinian physician-turned-revolutionary who'd become Castro's chief aide. His name? Ernesto 'Che' Guevara.

UK TOP 10 SINGLES

1: When
- The Kalin Twins
2: Carolina Moon
- Connie Francis
3: Return To Me
- Dean Martin
4: Volare
- Dean Martin
5: All I Have To Do Is Dream/Claudette
- The Everly Brothers
6: Fever
- Peggy Lee
7: Poor Little Fool
- Ricky Nelson
8: Endless Sleep
- Marty Wilde
9: Splish Splash
- Charlie Drake
10: Patricia
- Perez Prado

Grappling Irons Out In Fish War

In scenes reminiscent of a Hollywood buccaneer saga, Icelandic gunboats seized and boarded a British trawler today as it fished inside Iceland's new 12-mile limit, only to lose their prize - and the Icelandic seamen trying to take her into port - when a Royal Navy vessel used grappling irons to reclaim the boat.

While Icelandic authorities refused to take their men back from the trawler Northern Foam, the British Ambassador in Reykjavik received a protest from Foreign Secretary Gudmundsson at the Royal Navy's action, and more than 1,000 people staged a demonstration outside the British Embassy. It was the first incident in what would become a cat and mouse game, with Icelandic gunboats trying to move in on British trawlers which sailed away from Royal Navy vessels.

ARRIVALS

Born this month:

4: Mary Decker Slaney, US Olympic and World long-distance runner, holder of 22 US records between 800-10,000m

11: Mick Talbot, UK rock musician (Merton Parkas, Style Council)

12: Wilfred Benitez, US boxer, WBA welterweight and WBC light-middleweight champion

16: Neville Southall, Welsh international and Everton FC goal-keeper

19: Lita Ford, US rock musician, singer (The Runaways)

26: Kenny Sansom, English international football player

27: Shaun Cassidy, US pop singer

30: Marty Stuart, US country music singer, songwriter, multi-instrumentalist

DEPARTURES

Died this month:

11: Robert William Service, Canadian novelist and poet

22: Mary Roberts Rinehart, US novelist

SEPTEMBER 1

Surrey Become Seven-Times Champions

Already the most successful cricket team since the county cricket championship began in 1864, Surrey today reinforced their dominance of the English game when they won their seventh successive title.

Led between 1951-56 by Stuart Surridge, Surrey had been captained by Peter May for the past two seasons. With the dynamic bowling squad of Jim Laker, Alec Bedser, Tony Lock and Peter Loader in especially good form, Surrey cruised to victory over Sussex to take the championship - man of the match Bedser taking four Sussex wickets in a ten-ball spell.

SEPTEMBER 24

30 Die In Beirut As US Marines Begin Pull-Out

Thirty people were reported killed in the Lebanese capital, Beirut, today as sectarian violence marked the start of a withdrawal of US Marines from the city.

With the Middle East situation now in a state of uneasy stalemate, the decision to pull the marines out gave rival Christian and Muslim groups the chance to attack each other. With a complexity which would mark future events in Lebanon, members of different Muslim factions also fought, while the same was true of a divided Christian community.

SEPTEMBER 20

Martin Luther King Stabbed In New York Attack

American civil rights leader Dr Martin Luther King (pictured) escaped serious injury in New York today when aides managed to disarm a white woman who stabbed him as he made his way to a meeting with city authorities. Although clearly shaken, Dr King was said not to have been badly hurt - but it was the most alarming assault yet on a man who had become a prime target for those opposing racial integration.

Earlier in the month, the Alabama preacher had experienced more of the harassment which marked official opposition to his work. On September 3, he was arrested in the state capital, Montgomery, and charged with 'loitering'. Dr King alleged that arresting officers had used excessive force taking him into custody.

Two days later, a local judge fined him $14 (£5) for refusing to obey a police officer's order to leave the scene of his arrest.

Tension increased in Arkansas on September 12 when rebel Governor Orval Faubus defied Supreme Court orders to integrate state schools by closing all four Little Rock high schools.

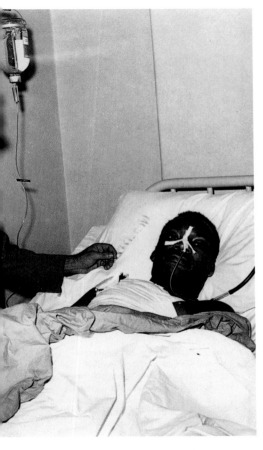

Hard-Liner Verwoerd Takes Over As South African PM

THERE NEVER WAS ANY optimism that the man chosen to succeed Johannes Strijdom (see August Departures) as Prime Minister of South Africa would offer much in the way of hope for the country's black population, suffering ever-diminishing rights and ever-increasing privations under the National Party's apartheid regime. But today's announcement that Strijdom's title was to be taken by Dr Hendrik Verwoerd shut out that hope for good.

Even by the severe standards of the National Party, Verwoerd was a hard-liner. After experiencing his inflexibility at close quarters during the eight years he'd just completed as Minister for Native Affairs, civil rights leaders knew that the 57 year old Verwoerd operated entirely with the unshaken belief that apartheid was the only way of life for South Africa. Born in Amsterdam, Verwoerd was brought to South Africa as a child, studied at Stellenbosch University and later occupied its Chair of Sociology. He resigned that post in 1937 in protest at South Africa's decision to give sanctuary to Jewish refugees fleeing Nazi persecution.

Founder-editor of *Die Transvaaler*, official newspaper of the National Party, Verwoerd opposed South African support of the Allies in WWII, and in 1948 was elected a senator. His Native Affairs appointment in 1950 effectively put him in charge of enforcing apartheid, a job it was clear he intended to carry on with increased authority.

EOKA Rejects UK Peace Plan, Resumes Violence

Violence returned to Cyprus with a vengeance today as EOKA terrorists rejected Britain's decision to implement its seven-year plan to allow political conciliation and reorganization, and launched a series of murderous attacks on military, police and civilian targets.

Two civilians were killed - one a Briton shot in the back outside a chemist's shop in Larnaca, the other a Greek Cypriot suspected of being an informer. His body was dumped outside a café by masked men. Four policemen were injured by gunmen, and two British soldiers were wounded when EOKA guerrillas launched bomb attacks on army lorries. The sound of sirens announcing a curfew was echoed by hundreds of car horns sounding the call-sign for 'Enosis', the union of Cyprus with Greece. Turkish youths began rioting in Nicosia on hearing reports of injuries to six Turkish women in inter-village fighting, while leaders of their community also rejected the British peace plan.

Hawthorn Pips Moss To Win World Motor Racing Championship

ALTHOUGH HE HAD SCORED only one Grand Prix win - the French, in July - to the four achieved by his great rival Stirling Moss, Mike Hawthorn (pictured) began today's final race of the season in Morocco knowing that the scoring system meant he could become the first-ever British world motor racing champion if he finished fourth, or better. While Moss won the race in his British-built Vanwall, attacking the circuit with the skilled aggression he'd displayed all season, Hawthorn's more considered second place for Ferrari meant he'd achieved his goal by a single point.

The first man to offer the handsome 29 year old champion congratulations was Stirling Moss, only too aware that while he may have captured the admiration of fans who loved his flamboyant style, he'd lost the championship to a safer, more accomplished driver.

It was a season bound to produce a new champion once the all-dominant Argentinian ace Juan Fangio decided to retire. What no-one anticipated then was a British title-holder, nor that British drivers would take the top five places. After Hawthorn and Moss, the next three names on the final honour board were those of Tony Brooks, Roy Salvadori and Peter Collins - the last-named tragically killed in the German Grand Prix on August 3.

Nobel Winner Pasternak Pleads Against Exile

Already expelled from the Soviet Writers' Union as a traitor for smuggling the manuscript of his Nobel Prize-winning novel *Dr Zhivago* to Italy for publication, author Boris Pasternak today appealed directly to Russian leader Nikita Khrushchev to reject Union demands that he be stripped of his Soviet citizenship and sent into enforced exile.

The 68 year old, who has already said he will decline the Nobel award, wrote to Khrushchev: 'I am tied to Russia by birth, by life and by work. Leaving my motherland would equal death for me.' Pasternak's novel - a story of frustrated love during and after the Russian Revolution - was refused publication by Soviet state censors for the way it depicted its hero's disillusionment with the regimes which followed. When it was published in the West last year, *Dr Zhivago* became an acclaimed international best-seller, the huge royalties from which its creator would never be able to receive.

UK TOP 10 SINGLES

1: Carolina Moon/Stupid Cupid
- Connie Francis

2: Bird Dog
- The Everly Brothers

3: Volare
- Dean Martin

4: King Creole
- Elvis Presley

5: Move It
- Cliff Richard

6: Born Too Late
- The Poni-Tails

7: A Certain Smile
- Johnny Mathis

8: When
- The Kalin Twins

9: Poor Little Fool
- Ricky Nelson

10: Mad Passionate Love
- Bernard Bresslaw

Jets Begin To Fly Trans-Atlantic

The inaugural flight of the new PanAmerican Airways Boeing 707 airliner from New York to Rome today, signalling the arrival of competition in trans-Atlantic jet passenger travel. A British Overseas Airways Comet introduced the faster way to fly 22 days ago when it launched the airline's London-New York service.

PanAm would increase the rivalry on October 28 with the start of regular flights between New York and Rome, and it would only be a matter of time before other carriers joined them on what all recognized as a vitally important image-enhancing route. Technically possible for some time, jet passenger flights only became reality when US authorities eased engine noise restrictions.

OCTOBER 28

Liberal Cardinal Roncalli Becomes Pope John XXIII

THE ROMAN CATHOLIC CHURCH made an astonishing switch in direction today when the 51-strong College of Cardinals elected the noted liberal Patriarch of Venice, Cardinal Angelo Guiseppe Roncalli, to succeed the ultra-conservative Pope Pius XII, who died on October 9 after a stroke. The new pontiff has taken the title John XXIII. In keeping with tradition, the news of Pope John's election after 12 ballots came at 5.08 pm with a plume of white smoke from the Sistine Chapel chimney. There had been confusion after the fourth vote when searchlights focused on the chimney in evening gloom had made the no-result dark smoke appear white. Vatican officials were forced to deny news agency reports which flashed around the world.

The sudden death of Cardinal Mooney of Detroit, only hours before the conclave went into secret session, reduced the College to 51 members. These included the exiled Archbishop of Peking, who was carried into the Sistine Chapel on a stretcher. For the first time ever, Italian cardinals were outnumbered two-to-one by other nationalities.

It is accepted that the new Pope owed his election to the votes of six French cardinals, many of whom he knew well from the seven years he spent in France as Papal Nuncio from 1946, during which time he incurred Vatican wrath by supporting the cause of outlawed worker-priests and became a close friend of General de Gaulle.

Patriarch of Venice since 1953, the 76 year old Pope - member of a poor farming family from a small village near Milan - continued to lock horns with the conservative Papal Court. His most recent brush had come earlier this year when the Vatican banned publication of a newspaper owned by left-wing Christian Democrat friends.

Greeted with an enthusiastic roar from the hundreds of thousands who had kept vigil in St Peter's Square during the drawn-out election, Pope John's appearance on a balcony gave him the opportunity to make a plea for world peace.

OCTOBER 31

Swedish Surgeon Makes Pacemaker Breakthrough

Fantastic news for the countless thousands of people in the world who suffer from potentially fatal irregular heart rhythms - in Stockholm today a Swedish surgeon successfully implanted the first internal heart pacemaker.

If Dr Ake Senning's breakthrough proves of long-term benefit to his un-named patient, cardiologists may have the answer to return those in their care to a more normal life, assured by the small electrical pulse which guarantees a regular and vital contraction of faulty heart muscles.

New Bubble Cars Burst Onto British Roads

While American manufacturers continue their love affair with the big, bold and brash in motoring design - and the spectacular new Buick on the General Motors stand was an undoubted hit with visitors to London's Motor Show, which opened its doors today - the battle for next day's headlines was won by the tiny new bubble-cars unveiled by the German companies Isetta and Messerschmitt.

Until now, the distinctive little machines had been three-wheelers. This year saw the introduction of four-wheel models from both market leaders, though the driver still sits alone at the front with one or two passengers behind.

Messerschmitt's new four-wheeled TG500 also continued the dual attractions of fantastic economy and safety. With a list price of £654 ($1,900), it delivered 52mpg and could not be overturned. For their part, Isetta offered a British-built 300cc three-wheeler for £350 ($1,000) or a four-wheeled German-made model for £676 ($2,000).

MICHAEL JACKSON - THE BOY WHO NEVER GREW UP

It is likely that future generations will remember Michael Jackson for the awful morass of scandal and rumour in which he's been trapped for the past few years - his bizarre, secretive and lonely lifestyle, the vast fantasyland estate behind whose walls he hid himself, his tragic attempts to change his appearance with plastic surgery, his admitted dependency on a cocktail of mind-numbing drugs, the allegations of impropriety in his friendships with young boys, and his marriage to the equally-troubled Lisa Marie Presley included.

Such a memorial would be tragic, for Jackson - born today in Gary, Indiana - must surely equal his wife's illustrious father as an entertainer who transformed the world of popular music to such an extent it's impossible to imagine it without him, or how it would be if he hadn't redefined it.

A star by the age of 10, as a member of the family act The Jackson 5, Michael was signed to his own solo deal with Motown Records two years later, and in 1977 moved to the giant CBS-owned Epic label to begin a solo career proper which made him a true international superstar.

Via multi-million selling albums such as *Off The Wall, Thriller, Dangerous* and *Bad,* a string of immense singles hits (*Billie Jean, Beat It, Thriller, The Way You Make Me Feel, Smooth Criminal, Another Part Of Me,* etc), a series of superbly crafted storyline videos and massively-successful world concert tours, he became one of the richest - and loneliest - people in the world, building a personal business empire which included ownership of The Beatles' catalogue of classics.

Then came the rumours, the scandals and the inevitable pulling back from live and studio work. Only time will tell if that is all there is.

OCTOBER 2
MARIE STOPES - THE WOMAN WHO SAVED WOMEN

Today's woman, who takes free advice on and access to birth control methods for granted, owes a huge debt to Marie Stopes, the scientist and social reformer who died today at the age of 78. It was she who, almost single-handedly, fought against the wall of ignorance which once made many women terrified of sex, and led to lives foreshortened by almost unending child-bearing.

Trained as a botanist at University College, London, with a PhD from Munich, in 1904 Stopes became the first woman to join the scientific staff of Manchester University. Prompted by the sexual failure of her first marriage, and increasingly aware that many other women were entering marriage unprepared and unaware, in 1918 she published *Married Love,* the first frank handbook on sexual matters.

The furore that caused was nothing compared to the row which followed *Wise Parenthood,* which advocated birth control in marriage to help limit family size and separate pregnancies. Thriving on opposition, and helped by her second husband, Marie Stopes used the royalties from her best-sellers to open Britain's first birth-control clinic, in north London, in 1921.

Followed within years by similar establishments in other main cities, all were eventually united as The Family Planning Association. Fittingly, its London headquarters is today called The Marie Stopes Clinic.

MAY 19
RONALD COLMAN - THE MATINEE MAESTRO

No-one raised a laconic eyebrow, smiled a seductive smile, or kissed a gloved hand quite like Ronald Colman, the British-born romantic actor who caused female hearts to flutter uncontrollably for the best part of 40 years, died in Hollywood today, aged 67.

Wounded during WWI, Colman drifted into acting, making his first films in England before moving to Hollywood in 1920. A natural first choice when it was decided to film *Raffles* in 1930, his sophisticated playing of the gentleman crook typified his easy style which was also captured well in *Beau Geste, Bulldog Drummond, The Man Who Broke The Bank At Monte Carlo, A Tale Of Two Cities* and *The Prisoner Of Zenda,* among dozens of others.

Justly awarded the Best Actor Oscar in 1947 for *A Double Life,* Colman made his last major movie appearance in Mike Todd's *Around The World In Eighty Days* in 1956, playing, as ever, a true gentleman.

Westerns Rule Ratings As America Goes Cowboy Crazy

WHILE PUNDITS PONTIFICATED on talk shows and sociologists scribbled learned articles trying to explain What It All Means About American Society, millions of their countrymen and women only knew they loved western drama series so much that, a year-end review of US ratings published this month revealed that of the 30 cowboy TV shows currently screened, five were established as the nation's most popular programmes.

Biggest new hit this year had been NBC's *Tales Of Wells Fargo,* starring former all-round athlete and WWII Silver Star gallantry medal winner Dale Robertson as the stagecoach company's troubleshooter Jim Hardie, a man who made sure the mail and the gold got through safely every week, come hell, high water and no-good sidewinders.

But Robertson's 'accidental' stardom (he nearly didn't audition, thinking there were already too many TV westerns!) was still only second behind *Gunsmoke,* the series which opened the floodgates in 1955, and made a household name out of its star, James Arness. As Marshal Matt Dillon, Arness strode the streets of Dodge City, rightin' wrongs, doin' what a man's gotta do, with his deputy Chester Goode (played by Dennis Weaver) a few limping steps behind calling 'Muster Dellon! Muster Dellon!'

Launched in 1957, but still riding high as the third hit cowboy series, was *Have Gun, Will Travel,* with the tall, dressed-in-black Richard Boone as the mysterious roving gunslinger Paladin, who quoted Keats, Shelley and Shakespeare, read Chinese newspapers and enjoyed vintage wine with his *haute cuisine.* The show's head writer, by the way, was Gene Roddenberry, who would go on to create the immortal *Star Trek.*

Fourth in the listings this year was *The Life And Legend Of Wyatt Earp*, a series which was initially launched before *Gunsmoke* but had taken this long to make the big time. Former marine drill instructor Hugh O'Brien (pictured right) played the man who actually had been the marshal of Dodge City in real life before moving to Tombstone and his final fatal showdown with the Clayton gang.

Destined to be a two-year wonder, the fifth western riding high was *The Restless Gun,* a show which was a spin-off from a character who first appeared in an episode of the CBS anthology drama series *The Schlitz Playhouse of Stars.* A working cowhand, Vint Bonner gave actor John Payne a chance to star, produce, direct, write and narrate tales of life in the rough 'n' ready west, and to own 50 per cent of the rights.

Two regulars in *The Restless Gun* were the giant Dan Block, who would go on to stardom as Hoss Cartwright in *Bonanza*, and Ray Teal, who became Sheriff Roy Coffee in the same long-running classic.

Meanwhile, waiting in the shadows down by the stables, where they'd emerge to become the biggest shows of 1959, were *Wagon Train* (with Ward Bond), *The Rifleman* (Chuck Connors with a longer gun) and *Maverick* (a gambling James Garner).

Still looking for an explanation? Maybe it's just that they were goshdarned good...

Government Launches Cheap Home Loans Plan

Good news today for Brits with an ambition to own their own homes: the government launched a new home-buying plan which included legislation enabling building societies to draw on a central fund and local councils to advance would-be purchasers 100 per cent of their new homes.

As illustration of the finances involved, the government literature selected a pre-1919 house, on sale for £2,500 ($7,500). Under the scheme, the purchaser would have to put down only £125 ($375) deposit and would be given 20 years to repay the mortgage at a fixed rate of 6 per cent. It was envisaged that while local authorities could advance the full purchase price, building societies would offer 95 per cent mortgages to successful applicants - making it easier for people to get mortgages on properties built after 1919.

UK TOP 10 SINGLES

1: It's All In The Game
- Tommy Edwards
2: Hoots Mon
- Lord Rockingham's XI
3: Bird Dog
- The Everly Brothers
4: Come Prima
- Marino Marini
5: A Certain Smile
- Johnny Mathis
6: More Than Ever
(Come Prima)
- Malcolm Vaughan
7: Carolina Moon
/Stupid Cupid
- Connie Francis
8: Move It
- Cliff Richard
9: Tea For Two Cha Cha
- The Tommy Dorsey Orchestra
10: It's Only Make Believe
- Conway Twitty

NOVEMBER 10

Speed Ace Campbell Sets New Water Record

Continuing in the steps of his father, Sir Malcolm Campbell, who became the first man in history to hold both the land and water speed records simultaneously when he broke the legendary American Gar Wood's water record in 1937, Britain's Donald Campbell smashed his own 1955 record speed of 202.32 mph on Ullswater Lake, Cumberland, today.

The 37 year old engineer playboy's new time of 248.62 mph would prove only the latest of an eventual seven record-breaking runs on his jet-propelled hydroplane.

He would also duplicate his father's double-record feat by establishing a new land speed of 403.14 mph on the Lake Eyre salt flats, Australia, in 1964. Like his father, Donald Campbell called his boats and land racers *Bluebird*.

He would die on January 4, 1967, attempting to break his 1964 water speed record of 276.279 mph. Just before his newest *Bluebird* was wrecked, Campbell had hit an unofficial speed of 328 mph.

Health Officer Warns Of Risks In Mother's Little Helpers

A FULL EIGHT YEARS before The Rolling Stones would be criticized for highlighting the problem in their song *Mother's Little Helper*, a senior government health officer today warned British women - or housewives, as he quaintly called them - of the dangers posed by increased consumption of sedatives, tranquillisers and stimulants.

The concern was expressed in the annual report on the state of public health by the Ministry of Health's chief medical officer, Sir John Charles, which said that while such drugs had been proved to be of benefit in the controlled environments of mental hospitals, their addictive qualities and potentially dangerous side-effects made their uncontrolled use hazardous.

Although agreeing that they could be used to avoid the anxieties of modern life, Sir John said that one true test of a mature personality was 'the capacity to face reality and tackle difficult situations with courage and determination'.

Some took this to mean that Sir John believed that those who fell back on prescription drugs were inadequate, a reading he was forced to defend and deny.

The report also criticized leading drug companies. Noting that new forms of tranquillisers were constantly being developed and introduced, Sir John added; 'The pity is that the energetic sales promotion devoted to the marketing of these agents is not always matched by adequate clinical trials'.

Quiz Show Scandals Kills $64,000 Question

Hit by the dramatic New York hearings in August and September which revealed that Charles Van Doren, the handsome and popular winning contestant in the top-rated TV quiz show *Twenty-One* had been fed the correct answers by its producers, the original and once-biggest TV quiz of them all, *The $64,000 Question*, was broadcast in the United States for the last time today.

The quiz scandal first broke in 1957 when Herbert Stemple, a *Twenty-One* winner, alleged he'd been ordered to take a dive so the more attractive Van Doren could win. Alerted by similar stories from other shows, the New York District Attorney ordered the formation of a grand jury. Amid a welter of lies and cover-ups, it was clear that most shows had been rigged in some way.

The networks pulled the plug, and audience figures on those which limped on sank like stones. The demise of *The $64,000 Question*, launched in 1955 and attracting an unbelievable 84 per cent of the entire US television audience at its peak, was inevitable. The death of a show which had once caused the Sunday night closure of cinemas and restaurants as America stayed home to watch host Hal March take contestants through the maze of increasingly-difficult questions in search of that legendary top prize, had only been a matter of when, not if.

Macmillan Opens Britain's First Motorway

BRITAIN'S FIRST STRETCH of motorway - the eight miles long Preston Bypass in Lancashire - was officially opened today by Prime Minister Harold Macmillan. After cutting a ceremonial ribbon and declaring the historic occasion 'a token of what is to follow', he was driven four miles along the six-lane carriageway.

Upgrading British roads and creating a much-needed motorway network was something Britain had been incredibly slow to take on. The concept was much more advanced in the United States, where President Eisenhower had encouraged many federal and state projects. Most European countries had begun to extend their major inter-city highways. And much of Germany's extensive autobahn system, it should be recalled, was built in the 1930s, under the guidance of Adolf Hitler.

All that said, Macmillan hailed the Preston Bypass as a 'symbol of the opening of a new era of motor travel' and said the government was determined to push ahead with what he described as 'an imaginative road programme'.

Unbelievably, the new wonder-road had been open for only a month when it had to be temporarily closed for repairs. Frost damage, before you ask!

Queen's Call Links Bristol And Edinburgh

Queen Elizabeth opened a new page in British telecommunications history today when she made the first call on a new dial-it-yourself phone system before throwing a switch to connect about 18,000 Bristol subscribers to the new service.

The Queen's call - watched by an anxious Postmaster-General, Ernest Marples, and an inquisitive Prince Philip - was from Bristol's main telephone exchange to the Scottish capital of Edinburgh, where the city's Lord Provost was waiting to speak to her.

The Post Office plans to connect all parts of Britain to the system over the next few years, enabling everyone to call long distance without going through an operator.

Nuclear Protesters Arrested At RAF Base

While leaders of the Campaign For Nuclear Disarmament have insisted theirs is a non-violent organization, a number of CND activists this month proved willing to risk jail sentences in their efforts to protest the arrival of nuclear rockets at British air bases. Choosing the RAF facility at Swaffham, Norfolk - the site of US-produced Thor missiles - they began a vigil outside the gates on December 6. Although there were clashes with RAF police the next day, the protesters stayed firm. Matters came to an explosive head on December 21 when a large force of military and civilian police descended on the CND camp. Although protesters offered no resistance, there were a few minor injuries reported, and the campaign ended with 21 people arrested and charged with obstruction, refusing to obey police instructions, or resisting arrest.

UK TOP 10 SINGLES

1: It's Only Make Believe
- Conway Twitty
2: Hoots Mon
- Lord Rockingham's XI
3: Tom Dooley
- Lonnie Donegan
4: It's All In The Game
- Tommy Edwards
5: Tea For Two Cha Cha
- The Tommy Dorsey Orchestra
6: Tom Dooley
- The Kingston Trio
7: Love Makes The World Go Round
- Perry Como
8: High Class Baby
- Cliff Richard
9: More Than Ever (Come Prima)
- Malcolm Vaughan
10: A Certain Smile
- Johnny Mathis

DECEMBER 21

Election Victory Gives De Gaulle French Presidency

BOLSTERED BY THE OVERWHELMING success of his Union for the New Republic Party in last month's national elections, when it won 198 of the 465 seats in the National Assembly, General Charles de Gaulle was swept into office as the first President of France's Fifth Republic today when more than 62,000 of the 80,000 members of the electoral college helped him destroy the challenge of his communist opponent.

The General, who will assume the presidency officially on January 8, received especially strong support in France's foreign territories, where many Communist and Radical-Socialist Party candidates failed to win a single vote, suggesting that the bulk of elected local government representatives in the electoral college had switched their loyalties to de Gaulle. One of his first appointments would be Michel Debré, who was moved from his post as Minister of Justice to become de Gaulle's first Prime Minister. A strong proponent of European unity, Debré took his new job only days before the Common Market Treaty came into force. He was notably keen that Britain should join the new group, if only to counter growing West German power and influence.

On the continuing Algerian crisis, de Gaulle outlined his policy of a negotiated solution. In a clear reference to recent allegations of torture made against French forces, he warned against what he called 'punitive or repressive measures' in the battle against the terrorism of Arab and French rebels.

On a less serious note, the new President - when asked if he was daunted at the prospect of governing - was quoted as replying: 'How can you govern a country which produces 265 different kinds of cheese?'

DECEMBER 6

Japan Introduces Super-Tanker Era

Like some giant science-fiction writer's dream, the world's first super-tanker - a vessel capable of carrying the equivalent of a million barrels of oil - was launched in the Kuri shipyard today.

Longer than three football pitches and taking more than three miles to come to a halt from full speed, the vessel is only the first of a number being built by Japanese freight companies to herald what many international marine experts believe is the dawn of a new age in transportation.

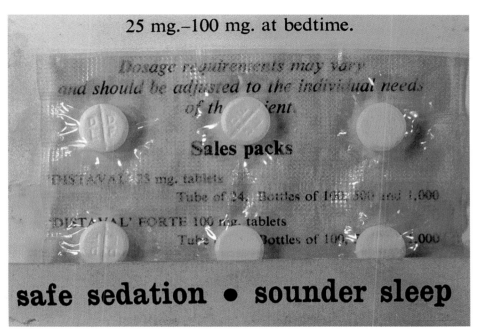

25 mg.–100 mg. at bedtime.

Dosage requirements may vary and should be adjusted to the individual needs of the patient.

Sales packs

'DISTAVAL' 25 mg. tablets
Tube of 24. Bottles of 100, 500 and 1,000

'DISTAVAL' FORTE 100 mg. tablets
Tube of 24. Bottles of 100, 500 and 1,000

safe sedation ● sounder sleep

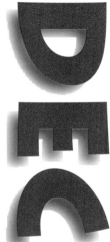

Thalidomide Blamed For Birth Defects

European child health experts today suggested that Thalidomide, a drug designed to relieve morning sickness during pregnancy, may be the common factor in what their report describes as an epidemic of serious defects in new-born babies during the past year. About 7,000 babies are reported to have been born with one or more limbs badly malformed or almost completely absent - most of them in Germany, where Thalidomide was originally developed and launched. According to the doctors, many of these extremely rare malformations appear to have been on infants whose mothers were prescribed Thalidomide.

Unlike most Western horoscope systems which group astrological signs into month-long periods based on the influence of 12 constellations, the Chinese believe that those born in the same year of their calendar share common qualities, traits and weaknesses with one of 12 animals - Rat, Ox, Tiger, Rabbit, Dragon, Snake, Horse, Sheep, Monkey, Rooster, Dog or Pig.

They also allocate the general attributes of five natural elements - Earth, Fire, Metal, Water, Wood - and an overall positive or negative aspect to each sign to summarize its qualities.

If you were born between January 31, 1957 and February 17, 1958, you are a Monkey. As this book is devoted to the events of 1958, let's take a look at the sign which governs those born between February 18 that year and February 7, 1959 - The Year of The Dog

THE DOG
FEBRUARY 18, 1958 – FEBRUARY 7, 1959
ELEMENT: EARTH ASPECT: (+)

Dog individuals are the most humanitarian, being givers who are prepared to sacrifice anything in life for those they love. Dogs were born to serve unselfishly, putting the needs of others first and themselves last.

Loyal to those they love, Dogs will always defend any member of their family or friends being attacked by word or deed. Equal rights and seeing justice done are of paramount importance to Dogs, who will always speak out on behalf of the less able.

Inevitably, Dogs' willingness to help can sometimes be misconstrued as interfering nosiness and being too ready to give advice that hasn't been requested.

But it is this essentially idealistic streak in Dogs' nature which makes them genuinely well-meaning people. Indeed, many turn their talents to voluntary or community work and will be tireless in their efforts to right injustice and inequality, and to improve the general lot of the less fortunate in society.

Dogs are solid, steady workers who put consistent effort into whatever they're doing, often to the point of obstinacy. But they rarely take on more than they can reasonably handle.

With their forthright honesty and humanitarianism, Dogs become respected members of society, trusted by all who come to know them. Loyal to friends and superiors, they will always make time to listen to people's problems, and the saying 'A man's best friend is his dog' sums up their dependability, loyalty and their apparent ability to find a kind word to say about everyone.

If Dogs do have a problem, it lies in their finding it hard to adapt to change, and many Dogs prefer to stick it out in the same situation rather than face facts and start over again. This may be because Dogs are innately pessimistic and inclined to expect the worst - a trait which can spoil their happiness. They will make changes if forced to, but tend to remain strongly nostalgic.

Another problem with Dog individuals is their tendency to live with an inherent inner anxiety. Though apparently composed on the surface, they have a deep-down sense of unease. But of all the animals in the Chinese zodiac, Dogs are the most unselfish, caring more about people than they do about money or personal success.

FAMOUS DOGS

Madonna
singer, dancer, actress
Mother Teresa
Nobel Prize-winning nun, nurse
Daley Thompson
Olympic decathlete
Sylvester Stallone
actor, writer, director
HRH Prince William

Michael Jackson
singer, writer, dancer, actor
Brigitte Bardot
former sex goddess, actress, now animal rights campaigner
Ilie Nastase
Romanian tennis ace
Liza Minelli
actress, singer, dancer